IND \|

D0906507

FEB 2 0 2019

ALL AROUND THE WORLD
CUBA

by Joanne Mattern

pogo

Ideas for Parents and Teachers

Pogo Books let children practice reading informational text while introducing them to nonfiction features such as headings, labels, sidebars, maps, and diagrams, as well as a table of contents, glossary, and index.

Carefully leveled text with a strong photo match offers early fluent readers the support they need to succeed.

Before Reading

• "Walk" through the book and point out the various nonfiction features. Ask the student what purpose each feature serves.

• Look at the glossary together. Read and discuss the words.

Read the Book

• Have the child read the book independently.

• Invite him or her to list questions that arise from reading.

After Reading

• Discuss the child's questions. Talk about how he or she might find answers to those questions.

• Prompt the child to think more. Ask: Cuba is a communist state. What kind of government do you have?

Pogo Books are published by Jump!
5357 Penn Avenue South
Minneapolis, MN 55419
www.jumplibrary.com

Library of Congress Cataloging-in-Publication Data

Names: Mattern, Joanne, 1963- author.
Title: Cuba / by Joanne Mattern.
Description: Pogo books. | Minneapolis: Jump!, Inc., [2018] | Series: All around the world | Includes index.
Audience: Ages 7-10.
Identifiers: LCCN 2017054179 (print)
LCCN 2017055568 (ebook)
ISBN 9781624969034 (ebook)
ISBN 9781624969010 (hardcover: alk. paper)
ISBN 9781624969027 (pbk.)
Subjects: LCSH: Cuba—Juvenile literature.
Classification: LCC F1758.5 (ebook) | LCC F1758.5 .M384 2019 (print) | DDC 972.91—dc23
LC record available at https://lccn.loc.gov/2017054179

Editor: Kristine Spanier
Book Designer: Michelle Sonnek

Photo Credits: Maurizio De Mattei/Shutterstock, cover; THEPALMER/iStock, 1; Pixfiction/Shutterstock, 3; dpvuestudio/Shutterstock, 4; rphstock/Shutterstock, 5; Frank Bach/Shutterstock, 6-7; Xinhua/Alamy, 8-9; Kamira/Shutterstock, 10-11; Olga Guchek/Shutterstock, 12 (left); Maks Narodenko/Shutterstock, 12 (middle); Max Lashcheuski/Shutterstock, 12 (right); Lester Balajadia/Shutterstock, 13; Jason Wells/Shutterstock, 14 (top left); Rostislav Ageev/Shutterstock, 14 (top right); Wang LiQiang/Shutterstock, 14 (bottom left); Sergey Dubrov/Shutterstock, 14 (bottom right); Patricia Hofmeester/Shutterstock, 16; akturer/Shutterstock, 17; JasonDoiy/iStock, 18-19; Kobby Dagan/Shutterstock, 20-21; DUSAN ZIDAR/Shutterstock, 23.

Printed in the United States of America at Corporate Graphics in North Mankato, Minnesota.

TABLE OF CONTENTS

CHAPTER 1

WELCOME TO CUBA!

Welcome to Cuba! This country is small. But it is the largest island in the Caribbean Sea.

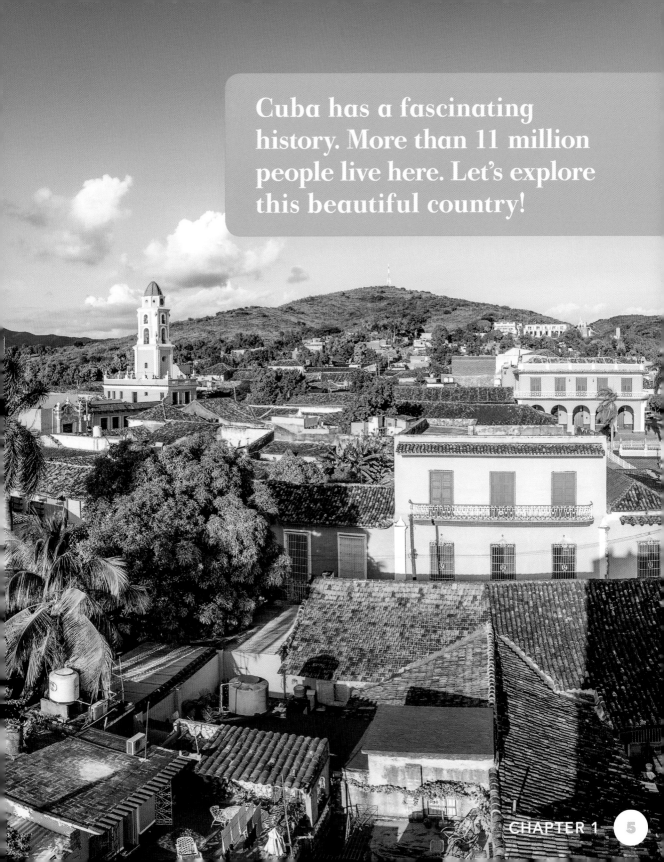

Cuba has a fascinating history. More than 11 million people live here. Let's explore this beautiful country!

Havana is Cuba's **capital**. It is the largest city. This city is an important **port**.

The Spanish **monarchy** once ruled Cuba. They built many of Cuba's cities. When? Almost 500 years ago!

Havana

TAKE A LOOK!

Cuba's flag was created during the Cuban War of **Independence** (1895–1989). Who was Cuba fighting? Spain. Each element has meaning.

■ = three original districts   □ = **purity**
■ = soldiers   ☆ = freedom

In 1898, the United States took control of Cuba. It became independent four years later.

Fidel Castro was Cuba's new leader in 1959. He ruled for almost 50 years. His brother, Raul Castro, was the next leader.

WHAT DO YOU THINK?

Two brothers led Cuba for more than 59 years. What leaders in your country have been related?

Raul
Castro

When Fidel Castro became the leader, he **banned** car **imports**. Most of the cars on Cuba's roads are more than 50 years old! The import ban was lifted in 2013. But many people here cannot afford new cars.

DID YOU KNOW?

Most people here make just $25 a month. A new car here can cost $85,000!

CHAPTER 2

A TROPICAL COUNTRY

Cuba's **climate** is perfect for growing fruits and vegetables. Which fruits? Papayas. Mangoes. Pineapples.

Hurricanes form over **tropical** oceans. They may hit Cuba during the rainy season. Palm trees here can withstand the winds.

crocodile

fish

bee hummingbird

hutia

Crocodiles and snakes live in the swamps. About 500 kinds of fish swim around the island. Look out for sharks!

Cuba is full of colorful birds. Parrots and flamingos live here. The smallest bird in the world is here, too. The bee hummingbird weighs less than a penny!

A **rodent** called the hutia makes its home in Cuba.

WHAT DO YOU THINK?

The air in Cuba is hot and **humid**. How do you think this affects the animals that live here? How does climate affect the animals that live near you?

CHAPTER 3

LIFE IN CUBA

Cuba is a **communist state**. The government controls almost everything. It decides what the businesses will be. It decides how much things cost.

Medical care is free for citizens. So is education. Children go to school six days a week.

Many people here have **service jobs**. They work in restaurants. Hotels. Stores. They also work as healthcare providers.

Many work on farms. Cuba **exports crops** like coffee and sugarcane.

What do Cubans do for fun? Many play sports. Baseball. Basketball. Soccer. Chess and dominoes are popular games, too.

Music is an important part of life. The rumba, mambo, and cha-cha dances began here.

Cuba is an amazing country. Maybe one day you will visit this beautiful island!

QUICK FACTS & TOOLS

CUBA

Location: Caribbean Sea

Size: 42,803 square miles (110,860 square kilometers)

Population: 11,147,407 (July 2017 estimate)

Capital: Havana

Type of Government: communist state

Language: Spanish

Exports: sugar, petroleum, fruits, fish, coffee

GLOSSARY

banned: To have officially forbidden something.

capital: A city where government leaders meet.

climate: The weather typical of a certain place over a long period of time.

communist state: A type of government in which all land, property, businesses, and resources belong to the government.

crops: Plants grown for food.

exports: Sells goods to other countries.

humid: Moist and very warm weather.

hurricanes: Violent storms with heavy rain and high winds.

imports: Products brought into a place or country from somewhere else.

independence: Freedom from a controlling authority.

monarchy: A government in which the head of state is a king or queen.

port: A town with a harbor where ships can load and unload goods.

purity: The quality of being pure.

rodent: A mammal with large, sharp front teeth.

service jobs: Jobs and work that provide services for others, such as hotel, restaurant, and retail positions.

tropical: Of or having to do with the hot, rainy area of the tropics.

INDEX

TO LEARN MORE

Learning more is as easy as 1, 2, 3.

1) Go to www.factsurfer.com

2) Enter "Cuba" into the search box.

3) Click the "Surf" button to see a list of websites.

With factsurfer, finding more information is just a click away.